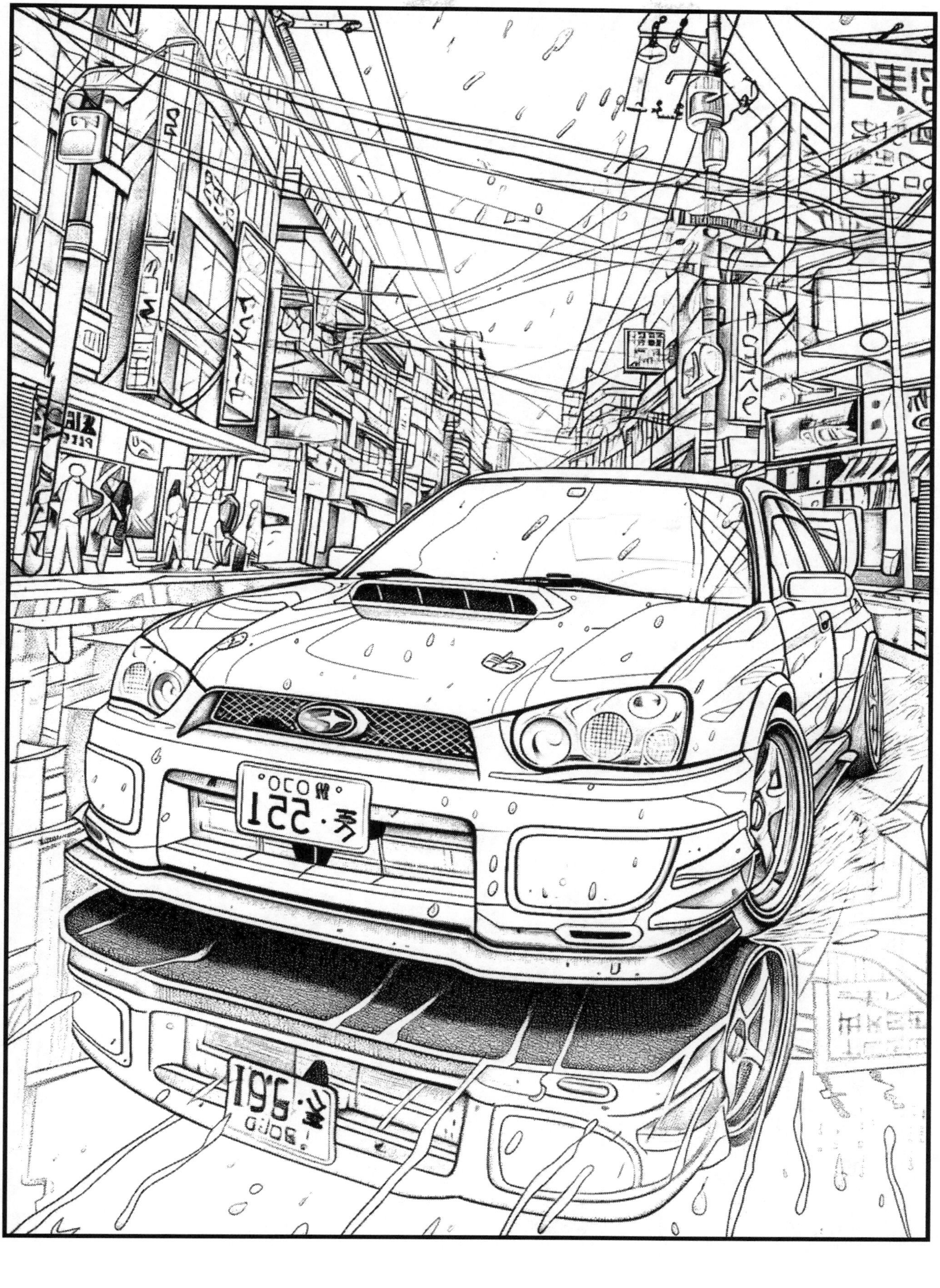

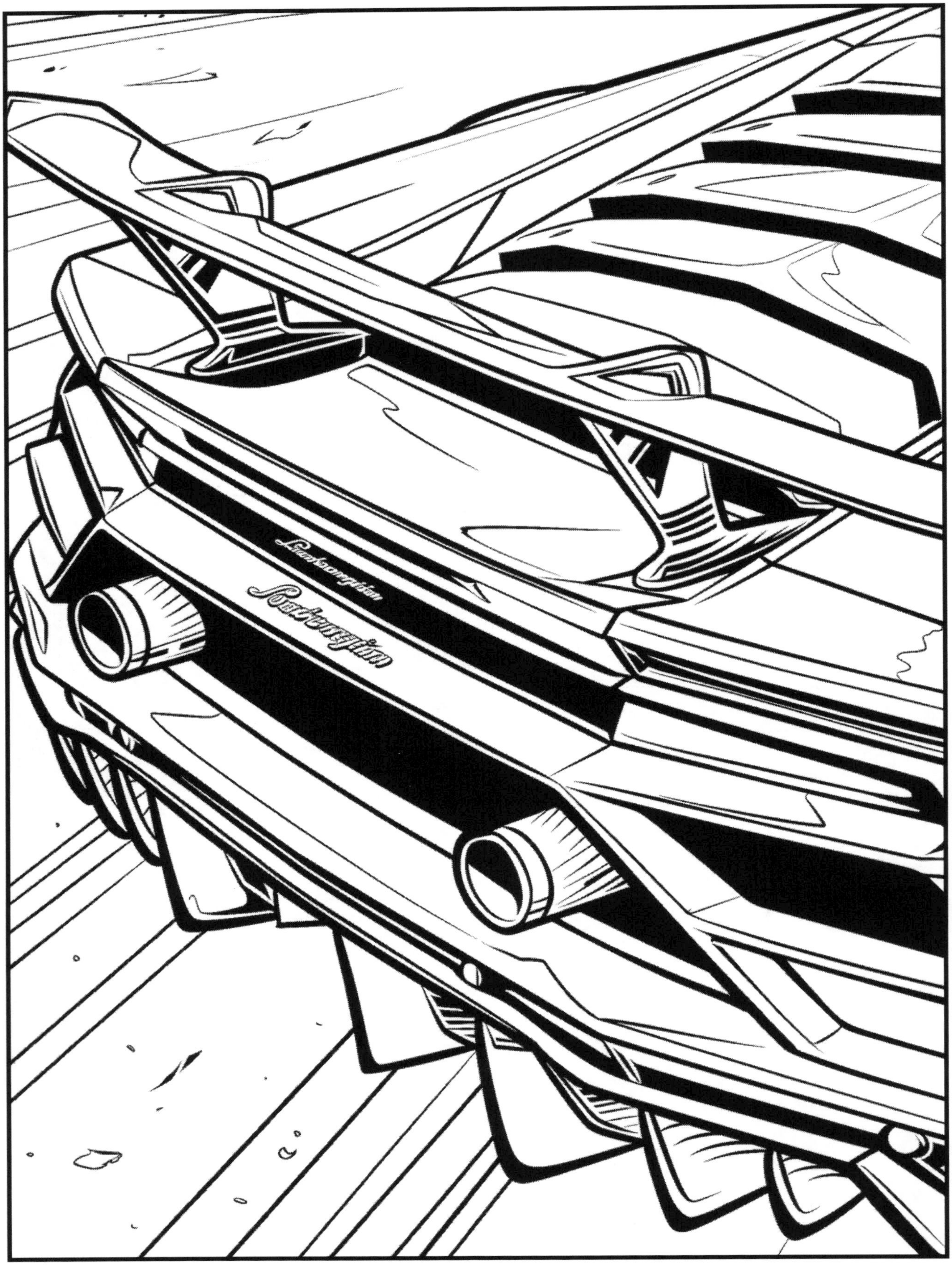

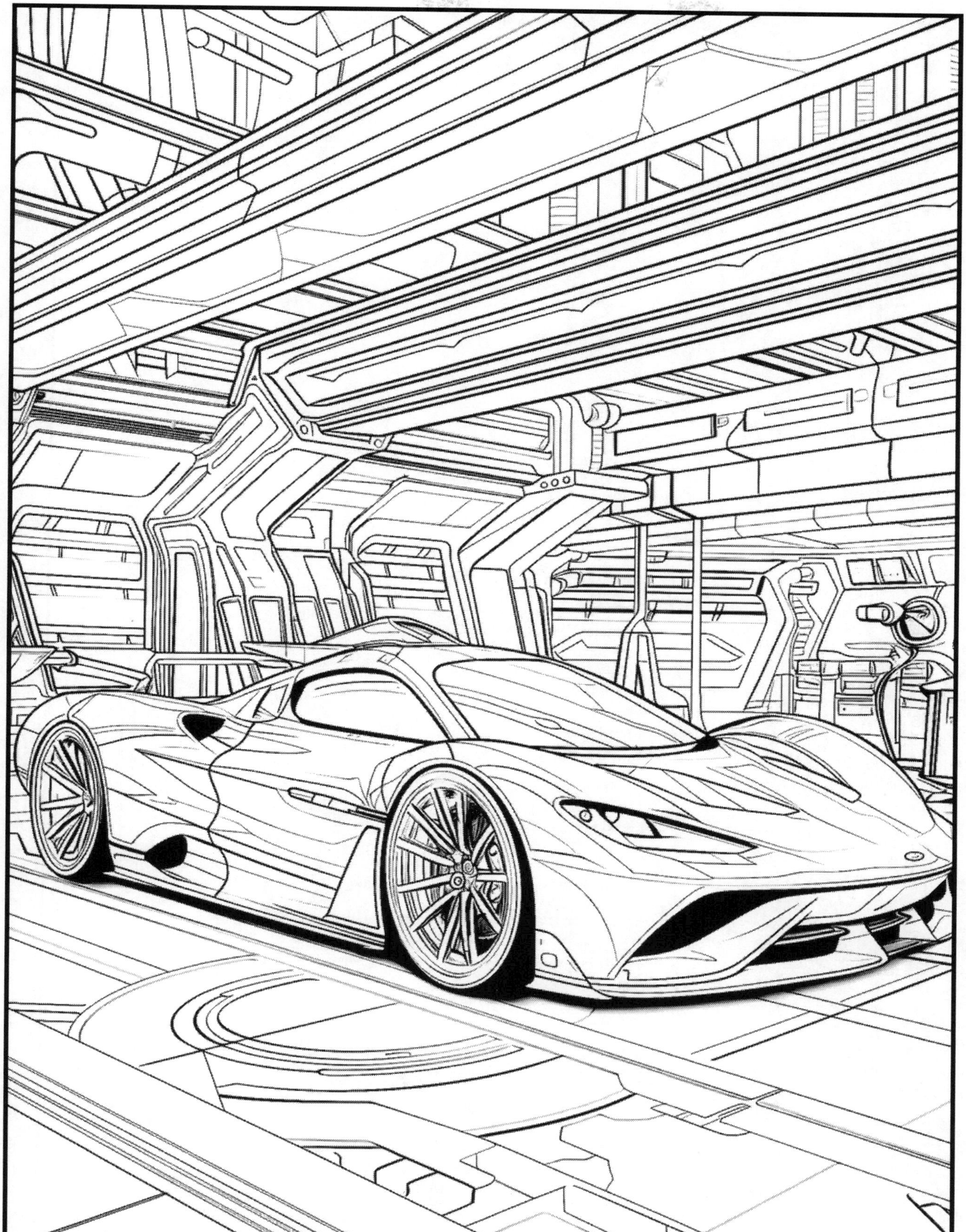

TOP
DOLE

HESEK

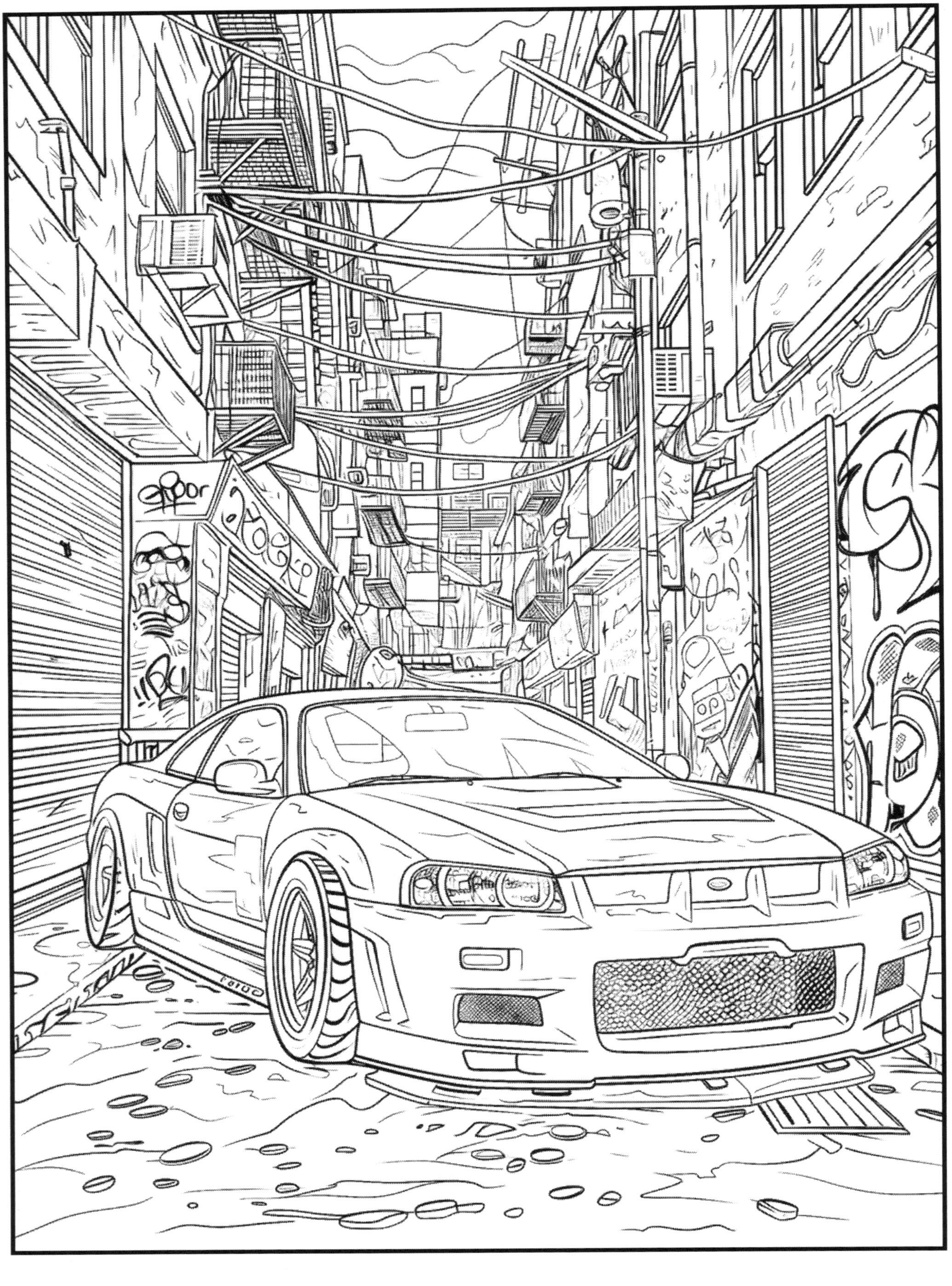

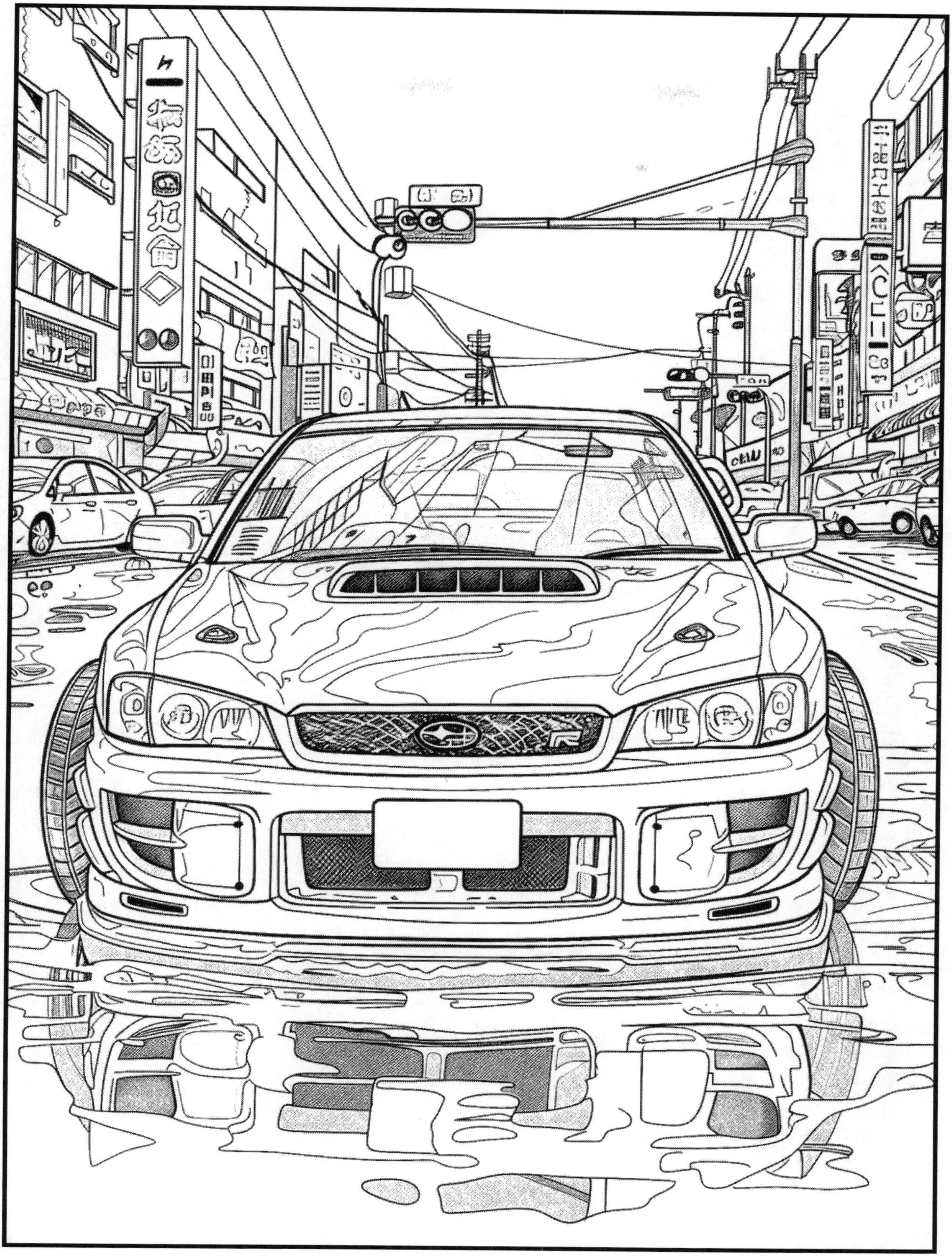

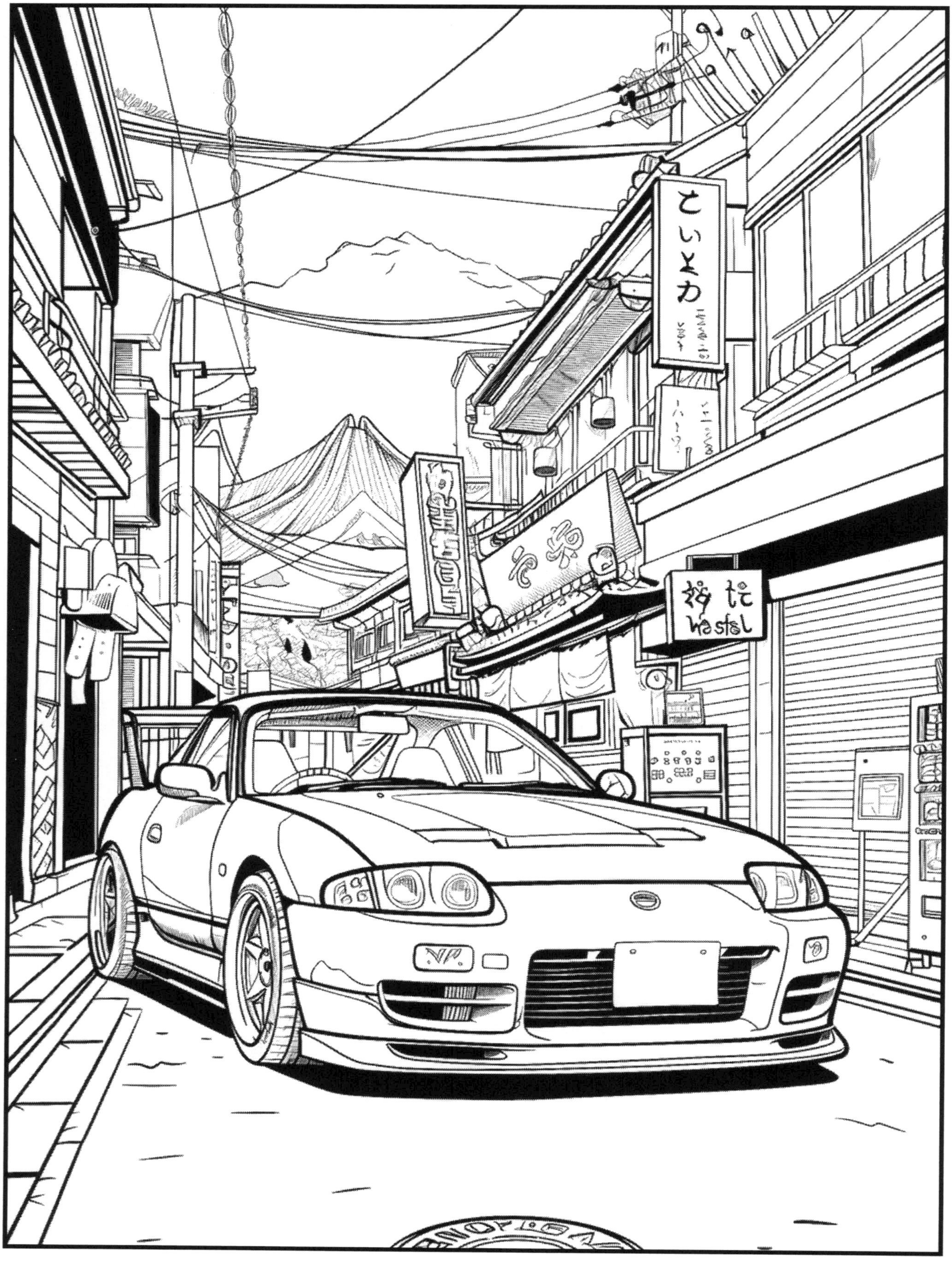

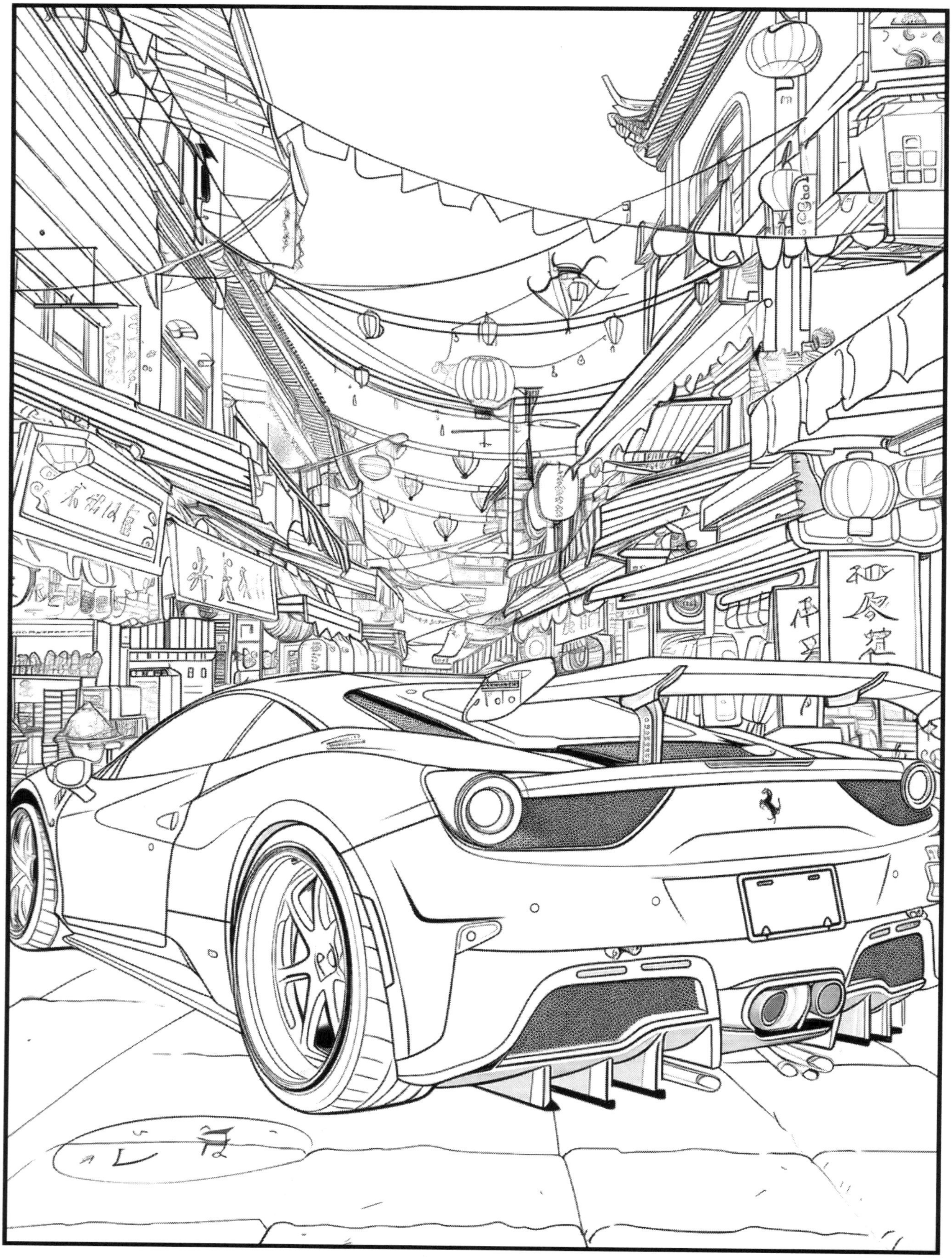

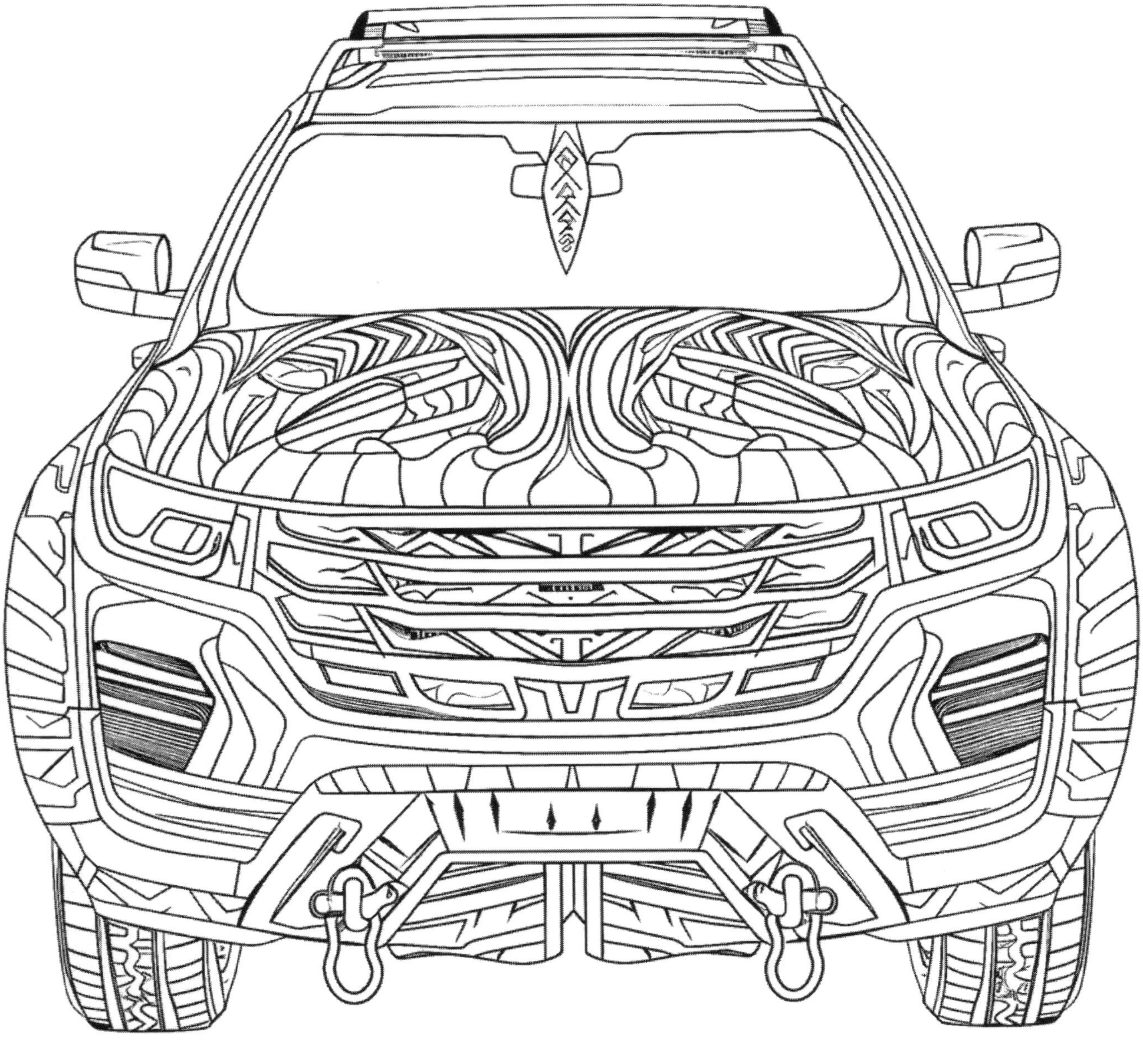

Made in the USA
Columbia, SC
18 October 2024

44670728R00028